Praise

It's the kind of book I wish my own children could have read when they were in grade school, a moving story that deserves a place in every school library in this nation. Told in straightforward, readable prose, *Fighter in Velvet Gloves* is the biography of an Alaska Native woman who, despite adversity, never gave up as she struggled for equality. Both Native and Non-Native young people should be able to identify with Elizabeth Petratrovich, who fought her battles in the far north long before the Civil Rights movement in the American South caught fire.

Joseph Bruchac
Abenaki Author and Storyteller, author of *Our Stories Remember*

This is a story that deserves to be taught in every school in the country. In a powerfully graceful telling, Annie Boochever, with Roy Peratrovich Jr., paints an indelible portrait of the woman who forged the trail for the civil rights of Alaska's Native people. The courage of Elizabeth Peratrovich takes its place in the annals of American history as a precursor to the civil rights movement fought in the South decades later.

Debby Dahl Edwardson
National Book Award Finalist, author of *My Name is Not Easy* and *Blessing's Bead*

From its apt title describing Elizabeth Peratrovich to the text outlining Elizabeth's life and civil rights advocacy, *Fighter in Velvet Gloves* is a wonderful and much-needed review written especially for young readers. However, young and old will appreciate learning more about Elizabeth beyond her famous and often-quoted testimony supporting the passage of the Anti-Discrimination Act of 1945.

Rosita Worl (*Yeidiklasókw* and *Ḵaaháni* in Tlingit)
Sealaska Heritage Institute president and assistant professor of Anthropology, University of Alaska Southeast

We Tlingit people are sensitive about our stories, yet Annie Boochever has delicately managed this conundrum and, with Roy, has achieved a respectful and deeply honest telling of Elizabeth's life. What I would have given to have had this inspiring book in my hands in my troubled youth.

Diane Benson
Assistant professor at the Department of Alaska Native Studies & Rural Development, University of Alaska Fairbanks

An inspiring book for our times, bringing to life real challenges overcome, and the enduring need to be vigilant to ensure rights gained are not erased.

Julie Kitka
President of the Alaska Federation of Natives

The ability to understand without condemnation,
to accept our friends and enemies in the light of their weaknesses,
is something we must acquire early in life
in order to find happiness in this world.

– Elizabeth Peratrovich
January 1957

FIGHTER IN VELVET GLOVES

Alaska Civil Rights Hero
Elizabeth Peratrovich

University of Alaska Press, Fairbanks

Text © 2019 Annie Boochever

Published by
University of Alaska Press
P.O. Box 756240
Fairbanks, AK 99775-6240

Cover and interior design by UA Press.

Cover image: Elizabeth Peratrovich, *We Can Do It*, acrylic on canvas by
Apayo Moore, 2014. www.apayoart.com.

Library of Congress Cataloging in Publication Data

Names: Boochever, Annie, author.
Title: Fighter in velvet gloves : Alaska civil rights hero Elizabeth
    Peratrovich / by Annie Boochever ; in collaboration with Roy Peratrovich,
    Jr.
Description: Fairbanks, AK : University of Alaska Press, [2019] | Includes
    bibliographical references. |
Identifiers: LCCN 2018028794 (print) | LCCN 2018049028 (ebook) | ISBN
    9781602233720 (ebook) | ISBN 9781602233706 (pbk. : alk. paper)
Subjects: LCSH: Peratrovich, Elizabeth, 1911–1958. | Tlingit
    Indians–Alaska–Biography. | Indians of North America–Civil rights.
Classification: LCC E99.T6 (ebook) | LCC E99.T6 B66 2019 (print) | DDC
    323.1197–dc23
LC record available at https://lccn.loc.gov/2018028794

Printed in the United States by Sheridan
November 2018

To TigerLily, Ayla Blue, and Harvey Dean

Table of Contents

Southeast Alaska.
UA Press.

Introduction

Native people thrived in Alaska for thousands of years before the first white fur traders arrived about the time of the American Revolution. By the end of World War II, the natural riches of Alaska—its great whales, fur-bearing wildlife, abundant salmon, ancient timber, and precious metals—had attracted wave after wave of newcomers. During that long period, the rights of Alaska Native people—the right to hunt and fish on their lands, to speak their languages, to practice their cultures, and to raise their children as they saw fit—were largely trampled, ignored, and, even worse, forbidden

Today, the majority of the largest Alaska companies are owned by Alaska Natives, and members of Alaska's 229 federally recognized tribes manage a statewide system of tribal health organizations, the largest in the United States. An extensive network of Native-run cultural institutions preserves and celebrates Alaska's eight distinct Indigenous cultures. Dozens of policy and educational organizations help protect and advance Alaska Native people's right to life, liberty, and the pursuit of happiness.

None of those things existed in 1911 when Elizabeth Wanamaker Peratrovich was born. Her generation of Alaska Native leaders planted the seeds of a civil rights revolution with their personal courage and commitment. This book celebrates all their efforts by telling the story of a woman who exemplified courage and commitment throughout her life. It is intended for middle school and high school students and their families.

Prologue

by Roy Peratrovich Jr.

I am the last remaining of Roy and Elizabeth Peratrovich's three children. This story includes personal details about my mother and our family that I have provided based on our family records and my personal recollections. In collaborating with the author, it was my hope to give the reader insight into not just the accomplishments of my mother but into who she was as a person.

Stella Martin, Yaan da yein, called my mother "a fighter with velvet gloves." Stella was a Tlingit Indian from Kéix' (Kake, Alaska). She was a champion of equal rights and a woman of great accomplishment herself. She was also a good friend of Mom's, and I think she got it right. When it came to fairness, justice, and the Alaska Native people, my mother was determined to stand her ground, but she would always do it with grace and dignity. The efforts of Stella, my parents, and many others came together on February 5, 1945, when my mother and father both testified before the Alaska Territorial Legislature in support of a bill to end racial discrimination in Alaska. Mom made the final remarks at the hearing.

Alaskans of all ages, Native and non-Native, stood shoulder to shoulder, some on chairs. It was only the second time in the history of America that a bill to end discrimination had come up for an official vote, and the federal Civil Rights Act of 1964 was still two decades away. Mom looked first to the gallery, then to the legislators behind their wooden desks. When she was confident she had everyone's attention, she began to speak. This is the story of how my mother came to give a speech that helped Alaska lead all of America in the battle for civil rights.

Fighter in Velvet Gloves

1

Elizabeth Peratrovich's Parents

On July 4, 1911, in the Southeast Alaska fishing community of Gánti Yaakw Séedi (Petersburg), Edith Tagcook Paul from Deishú (Haines) gave birth to the baby girl who would grow up to be Elizabeth Jean Peratrovich. Edith was a Tlingit woman of the Lukaax̱.-ádi clan of the Raven moiety. Elizabeth's father was William Paddock, an Irishman who ran a logging camp and local store in Tinaghu (Tenakee), a small community north of Petersburg.

But William and Edith weren't married. William was married to Edith's sister, Anna. Like many Alaska Native people at the time, Anna had contracted tuberculosis. White outsiders brought the disease to Alaska, and it was especially deadly for Alaska Native people because they had not been exposed to it before. After the custom of that time, Edith went to live at her sister's home to help care for William and Anna's children during the lengthy period that Anna was away being treated.

No one knows much about the relationship between Edith and her sister's husband, but we do know Edith became pregnant. Aware that she couldn't care for her

baby alone, Edith turned to the Salvation Army to find a home for her new child. It was there, we can imagine, that Andrew Wanamaker lifted the baby girl and cradled her in his arms.

His wife, Jean, gently kissed the downy black hair that covered the back of their newly adopted baby's head. "She looks like a little doll, don't you think, Andrew?"

"She's too strong to be a doll," Andrew replied.

Then Andrew and Jean took their daughter to their home in the town of Sheet'ká (Sitka), not far away, and that was how life began for Elizabeth.

Tlingit Elder Richard Stitt once said public speaking is "like waving a broom in a crowded room." It was easy for one's words to affect people in unintended, potentially negative, ways.

– Roy Peratrovich Jr.

2
Growing Up the Alaska Native Way

The word *native* means a person, plant, or animal belongs to a certain place. Three main groups of Native people live in Southeast Alaska: the Haida, the Tsimshian, and the Tlingit. Over thousands of years they developed cultures and a way of life especially suited to their Haa Aanî, or homeland. Andrew, Jean, and their new daughter, Elizabeth, lived what Alaskans call a subsistence lifestyle and followed many of the traditional Tlingit ways. It was a life that did not depend on grocery stores.

In the summer, Elizabeth followed her parents up the mountains to pick blueberries, salmonberries, and highbush cranberries. When they weren't berry picking, the family dug clams and fished for salmon, halibut, herring, and the oil-rich eulachon or candlefish. Elizabeth learned how to dry and can fish and to preserve berries to eat during the winter, and her father brought home deer, grouse, and ptarmigan from his hunting trips.

Elizabeth's parents spoke both English and Tlingit with their friends, but at home they spoke mainly Tlingit. Elizabeth quickly became fluent in both. Andrew's Tlingit name was Chalyee Éesh. Jean's was Shaaxaatk'í, and Elizabeth was given the name Kaaxgal.aat.

Understanding the meanings of Tlingit names can be difficult. Lance Twitchell, assistant professor of Alaska Native languages at the University of Alaska Southeast, says Andrew's Tlingit name, Chalyee Éesh, means "the father of Chalyee," which may mean "beneath the halibut." Jean's name, Shaax̱aatk'í, means "root of all women." Elizabeth's Tlingit name was K̲aax̱gal.aat, which may mean "person who packs for themselves."

Sometimes Elizabeth would join in at a K̲u.éex', a big celebration to honor the memory of someone who had died or sometimes to raise a new totem pole or dedicate a house. She would dance the ancient Tlingit dances through the night in her regalia–traditional clothing that featured a red and black wool robe with tiny, mother-of-pearl buttons sewn in the shape of a sockeye salmon, the crest of her clan. She might stop to enjoy a little smoked fish, gumboots, or her favorite, g'aax'w (herring eggs), all traditional Alaska Native foods. Then she would listen to the speeches. At every K̲u.éex', there were lots and lots of speeches, and Elizabeth liked to sit quietly, taking it all in.

The Tlingit people consider public speaking an important skill and one that requires careful thought. For thousands of years the Tlingits and other Southeast Alaska Native people did not use written languages. Instead, they told stories, made up dances and songs, and created intricate weavings, totem poles, and carvings to remember special people and events. In this way, Tlingit

Spruce root basket woven by Elizabeth's adoptive mother, Jean Wanamaker, circa 1941. *Peratrovich family photograph collection.*

history and important life lessons were passed from grandparents to parents to children.

Elizabeth's adoptive mother, Jean Wanamaker, was a renowned weaver whose work was later displayed at the Alaska Territorial Library and Museum. She taught Elizabeth how to dig, dry, and weave spruce roots into baskets so tight they could hold water. Elizabeth loved her Tlingit life. Andrew and Jean adored her, and Elizabeth grew up believing they were her birth parents.

TOP
Andrew Wanamaker
in Tlingit regalia,
circa 1906.
*Peratrovich family
photograph collection.*

BOTTOM
List of attendees at an
early organizational
meeting for the
Alaska Native
Brotherhood, 1912.
*Peratrovich family
photograph collection.*

3

School Days

When she was old enough to go to school, Elizabeth was surprised to find there were no Alaska Native teachers and speaking Tlingit was not allowed. Sometimes white teachers even made students kneel on rocks and struck them across their hands with a ruler for speaking their Native language. Another punishment was to make a student write on the chalk board one hundred times that he or she would speak only English.

As Elizabeth grew older, she was troubled to see that Alaska Native people and other minorities were separated in many ways from white people. Schools, hospitals, movie theaters, and even cemeteries had different places for people who were Alaska Native and people who weren't, and the nicest places were only for the white people. The reason for these inequities was racism, and young Elizabeth wasn't the only person bothered by it.

In 1912, just a year after Elizabeth was born, a group of Native people from around Southeast Alaska met in Sitka to form the Alaska Native Brotherhood, or ANB, and two years later, the Alaska Native Sisterhood, or ANS. Andrew Wanamaker was a charter member of the

ANB and an honorary founder of what is now known as the oldest Indigenous civil rights organization in the world. Both the ANB and ANS worked to advance Native rights throughout Southeast Alaska and to support improvements in educational opportunities, employment, social services, health services, and housing for all Alaska Native people. Later the ANB and ANS would prove essential to Elizabeth and her husband, Roy Peratrovich Sr., in the battle for civil rights.

When he was growing up, Andrew Wanamaker attended a boarding school that was only for Alaska Native children, the Sheldon Jackson School in Sitka. The school's founder, Reverend Sheldon Jackson, believed firmly in forcing Alaska Native students to abandon their traditional customs and practices, adopt Christianity, and speak only English. Reverend Jackson had been the chief education administrator in Alaska, and his mission to "civilize and assimilate" Alaska Native people persisted.

Andrew had no choice but to go along with this misguided approach to education, but in the process he learned some useful skills. Along with studying carpentry, American history, and English, Andrew learned about Reverend Jackson's Presbyterian faith. Later, he captained a ship he helped build for the Sheldon Jackson School, and the Presbyterian Church made him a lay minister. He and several others powered their boats— known locally as the "Presbyterian Navy"—up and down Southeast Alaska to preach to the local people.

When Elizabeth was old enough, Andrew brought her along on these trips. Since he spoke Tlingit and English, Andrew was able to deliver sermons in both languages. Many of the Elders didn't speak English at all in those days, so Andrew's language skills made him very popular.

In each village Elizabeth sat quietly in the back of the church, legs dangling from the pew while she listened to her dad's sermons. She was intent on learning everything she could and soon found that when she spoke seriously and chose her words carefully, people paid attention. Elizabeth could not have known that someday she would be an important speaker herself and would return to those same villages to minister about civil rights.

When Elizabeth was ten, her family moved to Lawáak (Klawock), a Native village on Prince of Wales Island in the southern part of Southeast Alaska. It was in Klawock that she met Roy Peratrovich, Lk'uteen. Roy's father was a fisherman and fishnet maker from Yugoslavia, and his mother was a Tlingit woman from the Klawock area.

Soon after, both Roy and Elizabeth were faced with a difficult situation. In those days educational opportunities in small villages like Klawock were limited, if they existed at all. Alaska Native students who wanted to continue their educations were forced to leave home to attend boarding schools. Sometimes children as young as five years old were taken from their parents and sent to those faraway schools. The disruption caused a deep sense of loss for families and communities.

The Wanamaker family, circa 1921. This photo was likely taken after Elizabeth's eighth grade graduation in Sitka, Alaska. *Alaska State Library. ASL-P492-III.*

The Presbyterian Church in Klawock where Andrew preached. *From the book* The Customs and Legends of the Thlinget Indians of Alaska, *by Oliver Maxson Salisbury, New York: Bonanza Books, 1962.*

Elizabeth went to the Sheldon Jackson School, the same school her adoptive father had attended. Only about a year later, however, she and her family moved to Kichxáan (Ketchikan), about 180 miles to the south. Meanwhile, Roy, who was two years older than Elizabeth, went to a boarding school called the Chemawa Indian School in Salem, Oregon, to continue his education.

Like the Sheldon Jackson School, Chemawa was authorized by the federal government to assimilate and integrate Native Americans into white society. Roy liked the more challenging academics at Chemawa and became captain of the football, basketball, and baseball teams. When he returned to finish high school in Ketchikan several years later, he was a seasoned athlete with a new sophistication that certainly was not lost on Elizabeth.

4

Citizenship,
a Terrible Sign, and Kayhi

Shortly before the Wanamakers arrived in Ketchikan, the United States Congress enacted the Indian Citizenship Act of 1924. The new law granted citizenship to all American Indian and Alaska Native people born in the United States or in U.S. territories like Alaska. Did this mean Elizabeth and other Alaska Native people would finally gain the same rights as white Alaskans?

Unfortunately, an ugly surprise awaited Elizabeth and her parents. A homemade sign hanging on the door of a popular general store blared "No Natives Allowed," and that was just one of many businesses that refused to serve them. Although the federal government now recognized Alaska Native people as citizens, the recognition did not make discrimination go away.

When Elizabeth entered Ketchikan High School, she was relieved to find both Native and non-Native students. This was largely thanks to Tlingit leader William Paul Sr., an attorney who brought a successful lawsuit against the Bureau of Education school in Ketchikan alleging that Native children were being forced to attend an inferior school. After the lawsuit, all students attended the same school, and everyone called it "Kayhi."

Elizabeth approached school like everything else in her life, with great commitment and enthusiasm. She wasted no time getting involved and even joined the glee club, where she sang in the operetta. Elizabeth was well on her way to becoming a woman who believed in being true to herself and fighting for it too. She sent this poem to a close friend shortly after she finished high school.

May 18, 1931

Hello Meallie,

Here's to the hope that you like my motto poem:

Do your stuff an' let 'em beller.
Do your stuff, and let 'em rap.
If you win, they'll holler "lucky."
If you lose, they'll holler, "Sap."
Let 'em help or let 'em hinder.
You shouldn't worry; do your stuff.
You're the girl you have to live with.
Be yourself and treat 'em ruff.

Lovingly yours,
Beth

Elizabeth Wanamaker and Roy Peratrovich Sr., high school graduation, 1931. *Peratrovich family photograph collection.*

Roy and Elizabeth finished high school together, and their relationship blossomed. After graduation, they both headed south to Bellingham, Washington, to attend Bellingham Normal School, now called Western Washington University. They wanted to become teachers.

5
Marriage and Klawock

Elizabeth and Roy were enrolled at Bellingham Normal School for only one quarter. They arrived in Bellingham in 1931, after America's worst-ever stock market crash caused a national panic that became known as the Great Depression. By the time they registered for classes, lines of people waiting for food handouts were a common sight across the United States. On top of that, a widespread drought forced farmers in many states to abandon their land, and eleven thousand banks did not have enough deposits to stay open. It was not possible for the young couple to borrow money for college during this difficult time.

Elizabeth and Roy knew their educations would have to wait, but their love would not. On December 15, 1931, they married in Bellingham and, soon after, headed back to Klawock.

During the next few years, Elizabeth gave birth to three children. Roy Jr. was first, then Frank Allen, and finally Loretta Marie, whom they called Lori. Meanwhile, Roy Sr. joined the ANB. While in Klawock, he served as a city policeman, chief clerk, and postmaster and was

ANB Convention
Roy Sr. (center)
and Elizabeth,
(left of center), 1940.
*Peratrovich family
photograph collection.*

elected mayor for four consecutive terms. Elizabeth spent most of her time caring for their children, but she also supported her husband in his efforts to help Alaska Native people. She became a well respected member of the ANS, having served for a time as grand vice president before being elected grand president in the early 1940s. Meanwhile, Roy had been elected grand president of the ANB, a position he would hold by unanimous consent four more times before he retired.

But Elizabeth knew they could do even more in the territorial capital, Juneau. So in 1941, at the age of thirty, she convinced her husband to move their young family to the biggest city in Southeast Alaska.

The Second Organic Act of 1912 created the Territory of Alaska, allowing for distinct judicial districts and the election of representatives and senators to a territorial state legislature. Alaska was not granted statehood until 1959.

Historic sign,
Front Street, Juneau,
circa 1943.
Alaska State Library.
Winter and
Pond Collection.
ASL-PCA-1050.

6

The Capital City

Juneau had 6,000 people in those days and was evolving from a mining town to a more cosmopolitan capital city. Moving there from the village of Klawock, with a population of about 450, was a big change for the Peratrovich family. In Klawock, nearly everyone was Alaska Native. Many residents were related, and everyone knew one another, so incidents of racism were rare. But in Juneau, and most other communities in Alaska with a sizeable white population, racial discrimination was common.

When they arrived, Elizabeth saw more hateful signs like the ones in Ketchikan. One screamed at her, "WHITE TRADE ONLY!" It was especially offensive because the Tlingit had been accomplished traders for thousands of years, navigating great river basins and mountain ranges from Southeast Alaska to the Interior.

Why would the young couple want to bring their family to live in such an unfriendly place? It helped that Elizabeth's adoptive parents, Andrew and Jean Wanamaker, had already moved there, but there was a bigger reason. As Alaska's capital, Juneau was the place where the future of Alaska Native people would be decided. Elizabeth's fierce love for her children and her desire to protect them gave her courage. She would work hand in hand with her husband and other Alaska Native leaders. Together they would do everything they could to end racism in their Alaska homeland.

But first they had to find a place to live. While walking up the hill behind what was then the Federal Building (now the Alaska State Capitol), they noticed several homes with "For Rent" signs. The homes were only a block from the Fifth Street School, and they appeared to be well maintained. It was a perfect neighborhood to raise their children. Roy Sr. called the phone number written on one sign and was told to come by the next day to complete the necessary paperwork so they could move in.

But when the couple got there, the owner said, "You're an Indian, aren't you?"

Roy answered, "Yes, I am."

"Your wife too?"

"Yes."

"Well, I'd like to help you, but other people who live around here don't want me to rent to Indians."

Elizabeth and Roy shook their heads in disbelief and left, more determined than ever to find a way to prevent this landlord and others from telling Alaska Native people where they could and couldn't live and raise their children. After much searching, they were able to rent a small house on Seward Street, also near the Fifth Street

School and directly across the street from the Federal Building where Roy worked for the Territorial Treasury.

Not long after they were settled, Elizabeth's adoptive mother became very ill with a kidney disorder. Roy Jr. remembers his mother's sadness when, soon after Thanksgiving on November 28, 1941, Jean died at the age of fifty-seven.

Roy Jr. said of his grandmother, Jean Wanamaker, "She spoiled me rotten, and I loved her very much."

And he told this story: Elizabeth was visiting her mother at St. Ann's Hospital in Juneau when Jean, after days of very little movement, suddenly sat up and called out "Ke-an-Kow," (currently, the preferred spelling is "Dikée aankáawu"), which means "the Creator" in Tlingit. At that moment, the back of the dark hospital room behind Elizabeth lit up. Then Jean lay down, never to awaken again.

"I believe that experience had a great effect on my mother. Maybe that was the beginning of my mother's work in Juneau."

7

Separate Schools

When they had finally secured housing in Juneau, Elizabeth and Roy Sr. discovered their children were not allowed to go to the school that was only a block away. Just like the stores with "No Natives" signs, Juneau had separate schools for white children. Alaska Native and other minority children were forced to attend Willoughby Avenue School, a government school in the "Indian Village."

The Native school had more students and fewer teachers, and Elizabeth believed it would not offer her children the kind of education she wanted for them. She also wanted her children to attend the same school as the other children in their neighborhood. Perhaps most important, she didn't think it was right to force any child into a separate school just because the child wasn't white.

Elizabeth went to the school district office and asked to see the superintendent, Mr. A. B. Phillips. No one knows exactly what happened at that meeting. Roy Jr. says his mother explained that the government school was too far away for her children to walk to.

Looking Down Dixon Street in Juneau, 1944. This is Roy Peratrovich Jr.'s first oil painting, done when he was 10-years-old. "My mother knew how much I liked to draw," he says, "so she found an art teacher for me. My teacher lived in the gray house. The building in the distance was the old territorial jail where they 'used to hang em.'" *Roy Peratrovich Family Collection.*

Elizabeth may also have mentioned that Alaska Native people were required to pay school taxes even though they were excluded from the public schools. Whatever she said, not long after the meeting, Mr. Phillips agreed that the Peratrovich children could attend the school of their choice, and Roy Jr. was the first Alaska Native child to attend the white people's school in Juneau.

Not everyone liked the decision. A headline in the *Daily Alaska Empire* read, "Board Chairman to Resign Rather Than be Party to a Board That Admits Indian Children to Public Schools." The article went on to say, "By admitting Indian children, it will lower the standards." Fortunately, with Elizabeth's help, the members of the board of education overruled the chairman. By 1947 Juneau schools were fully integrated. Several years later, one of the Native students, Judy Brown, graduated at the top of her class.

Roy Jr. remembers his time at the Fifth Street School fondly. He does not recall any overt racism there. He does say that he was not as well prepared as the other students after his time in the village school in Klawock. He worked hard, however, and quickly caught up.

8

The Native Vote

The period between 1941 and 1945 marked the United State's involvement in World War II and a time of great disrespect for Alaska's Native people. One of the worst injustices was the forced relocation of nearly nine thousand men, women, children, and Elders from their homeland in the Aleutian Islands to crude, overcrowded camps in old canneries and other dilapidated facilities in Southeast Alaska. The U.S. Army thought that destroying the Aleut villages would make it harder for the Japanese to invade that part of Alaska.

At the same time, the Alaska Territorial Guard, defender of Alaska's shores during the war, was composed almost entirely of Alaska Native volunteers. Elizabeth had a friend whose Native grandmother spoke only Tlingit but who nevertheless volunteered at the United Service Organizations, or USO, which arranged entertainment shows and care packages for soldiers. All the grandmothers' sons were serving overseas. Elizabeth herself wrote many letters to raise funds to support the American Red Cross in its nursing of wounded American soldiers.

But even though Alaska Native men and women were actively supporting the war effort, if a Native woman were seen in public with an American soldier, she was often taunted and humiliated. The army even issued an order that prohibited soldiers from "associating with" Alaska Native women. That meant a Native soldier could be punished for speaking in public to his own mother or sister.

This kind of discrimination was widespread and continued well after the war was over. Elizabeth later heard about Alberta Schenck, a seventeen-year-old high school student in Nome whose father was a white army veteran of World War I and whose mother was an Alaska Native woman of Iñupiat descent. In early 1944 Alberta was fired from her position as an usher at Nome's Dream Theater for speaking out about the theater's segregated seating.

In response, she wrote an essay about the seating policy that appeared in the *Nome Nugget.* A short time later, while on a date with a white army sergeant, Alberta sat in the whites only section of the theater. She was arrested and spent a night in jail.

Finally, Alaska Native soldiers were dying on the battlefield for America, but their family members could be prevented from voting. Even though they were U.S. citizens, Alaska Native people sometimes had to pass special voting tests, including a literacy test. The tests were in English, but many of the Elders were much more comfortable with their traditional languages. Because the Elders in Southeast Alaska grew up under Russian rule,

The "Toilet Paper Defense"
The practice of making it difficult for Alaska Natives to vote had a long history. In 1922 the Alaska Native attorney, William Paul Sr., defended a Tlingit Elder named Charlie Jones who had been arrested for voting illegally. Jones was also known as Chief Shakes VII and was a leader of the Stikine area in Southeast Alaska. Paul's mother, Matilda "Tilly" Paul Tamaree, was also arrested for aiding and abetting Jones. At the trial in Ketchikan, Paul was able to prove that even though Charlie Jones lived an Alaska Native lifestyle and spoke only Tlingit, he owned a home, paid taxes, used a knife and fork, and—Paul noted pointedly—used toilet paper rather than tree leaves for personal hygiene like any civilized person. Paul won the case, but even when full citizenship was granted to Alaska Natives and American Indians in 1924, efforts to deny the vote to Indigenous Americans continued.

many spoke not only their Native language but Russian as well. Nevertheless, under the law at that time, they were considered illiterate and ineligible to vote.

Meanwhile, the ANB and ANS, along with people like Elizabeth, Roy Sr., William Paul Sr., many other Alaska Native leaders, and some white supporters continued to work for equality in Alaska. One of their most important allies turned out to be the territorial governor, Ernest Gruening.

Ernest Gruening was appointed as Territorial governor of Alaska by President Franklin D. Roosevelt in 1939. Gruening did not like prejudice and discrimination. He had seen plenty of injustice as a boy growing up in New

Anthony Dimond,
territorial congressional
representative,
circa 1943.
Alaska State Library.
ASL-P523-15.

York City, and although he had found personal success as a doctor, journalist, and politician, he was Jewish and had felt the sting of prejudice firsthand. Elizabeth and Roy Sr. sent a letter to the new governor urging him to have the hateful signs removed and asking for his help battling other discriminatory practices.

Governor Gruening was sympathetic to their cause. Although he was unsuccessful in removing the signs, he worked closely with Anthony Dimond (Alaska's territorial representative in Congress) and others, including Elizabeth and Roy Sr., to draft an anti-discrimination bill and present it to the Alaska Territorial Legislature in 1943. At that time, however, the legislature was dominated by white men who represented business interests outside Alaska. The equality of Alaska Natives was not a priority for them, and although the bill passed in the House, it suffered a bitter defeat in the Senate. In those days the legislature met only every other year, so it would be 1945 before the bill could be reconsidered.

It was clear to Elizabeth that to pass an anti-discrimination bill, support was needed from all over Alaska, not just Juneau. She set up a meeting with Governor Gruening to come up with a plan.

Governor Gruening references several meetings with both Elizabeth and Roy Sr. in his book, *Many Battles: The Autobiography of Earnest Gruening.*

Gruening does not describe exactly what was said. The imagined conversation in chapter 9 reflects the substance of their meeting based on the book and on Roy Jr.'s recollections of later conversations with his mother.

9

Meeting with the Governor

The day of the meeting, Roy Sr. had to be at work, so Elizabeth put on her best suit, the green one, complete with a hat and soft brown gloves, and set off on her own. After being greeted warmly by the governor, she got right to the point.

"Governor, Roy and I feel we have done all we can here in Juneau. The ANS and ANB are committed to passing an anti-discrimination bill, and many non-Native citizens have promised support, but we need help from all over the territory to convince the legislature."

Governor Gruening leaned back in his chair and nodded. "You are absolutely right. You could start by recruiting more Alaska Natives to run for office. William Paul Sr. was the only Alaska Native in the legislature, but he lost his third run back in 1928."

Elizabeth nodded, "Yes, but electing enough Alaska Natives will take time. My son, Roy Jr., will be old enough to vote by then."

The governor smiled. "Together we can do this. I'll see if I can get the government in Washington, DC, to increase the size of our legislature. That will make it harder for a few bad apples to sway the vote. I know your husband can't leave his job, but could you arrange to travel around Southeast Alaska and speak to your people? Ask them to organize more ANB and ANS camps too."

Elizabeth hesitated, "I think people will listen to me, but I don't have money for airplanes, and I have three children to take care of."

They sat quietly for a moment. Elizabeth shifted in her seat, then said, "I wonder if Shell Simmons, the owner of Alaska Coastal Airlines, would help? Everybody knows him, but I've never actually talked to him."

Governor Gruening looked at Elizabeth directly and said, "His planes fly all around Southeast. I bet he'd take you along when there's an empty seat. Go see him, and if he gives you a hard time, ask him to call me."

Sheldon "Shell" Simmons was key to the plan. Most of the towns in Southeast Alaska are on islands and not connected by roads. In Elizabeth's day, there was no system of government-run ferries as there is now. If people didn't own a boat, they would hitch rides with fishermen. If they were in a hurry and could afford it, they took floatplanes like the Grumman Goose that Shell Simmons flew.

Elizabeth followed Governor Gruening's advice and found Shell down on the wharf where his planes were tied up. Shell was sympathetic and quickly agreed to help.

It was about this time that Elizabeth made a discovery that affected her deeply. Besides all her volunteer work to gain support for the anti-discrimination bill, she also worked as a secretary in the territorial legislature. Leaving the office one day, Elizabeth noticed an elderly Tlingit woman who appeared to be watching her. She didn't think much of it at first, but the woman was there every day. Finally, Elizabeth decided to approach her, but the next day when she left work at the usual time, the woman was nowhere to be seen.

That afternoon at home, the phone rang. It was the Presbyterian minister, Reverend Walter Soboleff. The conversation went something like this:

"Elizabeth, it is with great sadness that I must tell you, your birth mother just passed away."

After a moment of silence, Elizabeth responded, "There must be some mistake. My mother, Jean Wanamaker, passed away in Juneau two years ago, in 1941."

"Elizabeth, I'm talking about your birth mother, Edith Tagcook Paul. Jean was your adoptive mother."

Elizabeth soon realized the woman who had been watching her every day was her birth mother. If only she had spoken to her sooner!

Elizabeth was greatly saddened, but she would not let her personal loss derail the important work she knew she had to do. Summers are short in Alaska. There was no time to waste.

True to her name, Minnie wasn't much taller than I,
but what she lacked in height, she more than made up for in
width. And she was one of the kindest adults I ever knew.

–Roy Peratrovich Jr.

Minnie Field and the
Orphanage in Juneau
near Tee Harbor,
circa 1944.
Alaska State Library.
Minnie Field family
photo collection.
ASL-p35-[208-232].

10

The Orphanage

With the governor's support and a pilot willing to fly her for free, Elizabeth could get to work. Although large by floatplane standards, the Grumman Goose only carried six or seven passengers, and Shell could only spare one seat for Elizabeth. Fortunately, Lori was still small enough to fit on Elizabeth's lap, so she got to go along for the ride. But what about the boys?

On the outskirts of Juneau, seventeen dirt-road miles north of Governor Gruening's office, was a small orphanage, the Minfield Home. Elizabeth knew Minnie Field, the woman who ran it. Minnie was a kind woman, and she agreed to care for the boys during Elizabeth's summer of traveling and working for passage of the anti-discrimination bill. Frank was six then, and Roy Jr. nine. The boys had never been away from home before. What began as a frightening separation turned out to be a time Roy Jr. remembers fondly as Minnie welcomed them into what she thought of as her family. Roy Jr. and Frank missed being at home with their parents and sister, and Roy, Elizabeth, and Lori missed them too. But the boys seemed to understand their mother was doing something important.

11

Laying the Groundwork by Airplane

All summer whenever Shell Simmons had an empty seat in his plane, he invited Elizabeth to join him. She worked her magic in every town in Southeast. She even donned mukluks and a fur parka to travel, first by plane and then by dog team, to some villages way up north. Decades later, when Elizabeth's grandson Mike went hunting near Deering in the Northwest Arctic Borough, he found the people there still remembered his grandmother's visit.

In her quiet, no-nonsense way, Elizabeth would explain why the anti-discrimination bill would help Alaska Native people, why it was so important for them to vote, and why they should consider running for office. Elizabeth's message was met with great enthusiasm. One added result was that many more villages started their own ANB and ANS camps.

Meanwhile, Governor Gruening worked his own kind of magic. He helped Congressman Dimond convince Congress to amend the Alaska Organic Act, which increased the size of the territorial legislature. That, coupled with a reapportionment bill to change the way voting districts were laid out, resulted in an

Shell Simmons,
circa 1944.
Alaska State Library.
Shell Simmons family
photo collection.
ASL-P356-1028.

opportunity for fairer representation. The influence of outside special interests that had dominated the legislature in previous years was diminished, and new legislative seats became available for Alaska Native candidates to fill.

Roy Sr.'s older brother Frank, from Klawock, and Andrew Hope, a Tlingit boat-builder from Sitka, ran for seats in the House of Representatives and won. In Northwest Alaska, Percy Ipalook, an Iñupiat Eskimo and Presbyterian minister from Wales, was elected first to the Alaska House of Representatives and later to the Alaska Senate. Change was in the air!

My mother never stopped trying to correct a wrong.
I remember driving with her each Thanksgiving and
Christmas to deliver food to needy families.

– Roy Peratrovich Jr.

Sketch of Governor
Gruening by
Roy Peratrovich Jr.,
circa 1944.
Peratrovich family
photograph collection.

12

Grand Presidents

By this time, the Peratrovichs felt like full-fledged members of the Juneau community. After the busy summer of 1943, the family moved in with Elizabeth's father. Alone now, Andrew was grateful for the company.

Little Frank joined Roy Jr. at the Fifth Street School, where Roy Jr. was discovering art, which would become a great passion for him throughout his life.

The family home became a hub for all sorts of guests. Stray cats often found a safe haven there, and for a while Roy Jr.'s friends would gather after school to listen to his mother read Victor Hugo's *Hunchback of Notre Dame*. One Thanksgiving Roy Jr. found himself climbing over and around the sleeping forms of a dozen well-fed basketball players from Sitka to get upstairs to his room.

When Elizabeth wasn't entertaining or rallying for civil rights, Roy Jr. would often find her sitting at the kitchen table in the evening with her hair piled up on her head and knitting needles clicking as she and his father talked about how to improve the lives of their people.

Some nights, he'd hear the steady tap-tap-tap of the typewriter instead. He would later learn his parents had been composing letters to raise awareness of the injustices faced by their people. Their targets included the local newspaper, Governor Gruening, Congressman Dimond, the army, the local judiciary, the attorney general, and the U.S. Department of the Interior Office of Indian Affairs. In late 1944 Elizabeth even wrote to the Office of the Solicitor in the Department of the Interior to ask whether Alaska Natives could be compensated in money for the loss of their aboriginal rights to land. The answer would come a quarter century later with passage of the Alaska Native Claims Settlement Act.

But while Elizabeth and her family enjoyed their time at home, racism was still a dark cloud over Alaska. Roy Jr. took a job delivering newspapers. One day a man who worked at the newspaper office called him "a little Siwash boy." Not knowing what that meant, he mentioned it to his parents. It wasn't until years later he found out the word *Siwash* was hurtful slang for someone who has both Alaska Native and European ancestors. That incident must have infuriated Elizabeth and Roy Sr.

The Peratrovichs' influence grew. They were well-known leaders in the ANB's and ANS's fight for equality, with Elizabeth at the helm of the ANS as grand president and Roy Sr. serving as grand president of the ANB. The couple had become an effective political team.

The legislature would soon hold a hearing on the anti-discrimination bill, and the legislators would certainly question Roy Sr. in detail because of his position in the ANB. Roy thought it was likely no one else would be asked to speak, but since Elizabeth was the grand president of the ANS, they decided she should make a closing presentation. They planned their testimony carefully. Just as Elizabeth's father had prepared for his Sunday sermons, Elizabeth and Roy Sr. spent long hours around the kitchen table working out what she would say.

13

The Big Day

February 5, 1945, began with a change in the weather. The fifty-knot winds that had buffeted the temperature down to barely zero retreated down Gastineau Channel and up over the Taku Glacier. Heavy, wet snow smothered the mountains, and a gray mist slowly enveloped the town. As the weather warmed, so did the anti-discrimination debate.

The legislative gallery was so crowded the doors were flung open, and people lined the hallway outside. Some stood on chairs to see better. Elizabeth sat in the back, knitting needles clicking, with little Lori feeding her the yarn.

Edward Anderson, the former mayor of Nome, had introduced the anti-discrimination bill in the House of Representatives earlier that day. Support for the bill had been strengthening, helped by Alberta Schenck's continued advocacy and that of Alberta's aunt, Frances Longley, a member of the ANS in Nome and the longtime partner of Senator O. D. Cochran of Nome. The newly elected Alaska Native representatives, Frank Peratrovich and Andrew Hope, joined with a group of others who

The testimony Elizabeth and others gave to the territorial senate that day in 1945 was not officially recorded. At that time, minutes were not taken at public hearings. Remarks attributed to specific legislators are taken from *A Recollection of Civil Rights Leader Elizabeth Peratrovich, 1911–1958*, compiled by the Central Council of Tlingit and Haida Indian Tribes of Alaska.

were committed to equality, and the bill passed the House easily with a vote of nineteen to five.

Senate approval was less certain. Senator Cochran and Senator Norman Ray "Doc" Walker spoke in favor of passage, but the senate was a smaller body with no Alaska Native members and some fierce opponents of the bill. Intense arguing and bickering erupted. A senator from Juneau, Allen Shattuck, exclaimed, "Far from being brought closer together, which will result from this bill, the races should be kept further apart. Who are these people, barely out of savagery, who want to associate with us whites with five thousand years of recorded civilization behind us?"

Elizabeth's knitting needles froze. She drew a slow, deliberate breath before beginning to knit again.

Senator Frank Whaley, a bush pilot and gold miner from Fairbanks, called the bill "a lawyer's dream and a natural in creating hard feelings between whites and Natives." He went on to say, "I don't want to sit next to an Eskimo in a theater, because they smell."

The words grew even nastier.

Senator Grenold Collins said, "It is the mixed breed who is not accepted by either race who causes the trouble."

According to Cecelia Kunz, a good friend of Elizabeth's and a Tlingit member of the ANS who was present that day, one senator was so angry he jumped up, knocking his chair over, and stomped out. Heated debate from both sides continued. Just as Roy and Elizabeth had anticipated, Senator Doc Walker asked Roy Sr. to speak as the ANB grand president.

Roy Sr. testified that there was no question discrimination against Alaska Natives existed, and he reminded the crowd of the powerful display of harmful words and comments they had just heard from certain members of the senate. He went on to thank Governor Gruening for his support of the bill and explained how only Alaska Natives can know how it feels to be discriminated against in this, their own homeland.

And that ended the planned testimony on the bill.

Governor Gruening signs the Anti-Discrimination Act of 1945 with O. D. Cochran, Elizabeth Peratrovich, Edward Anderson, Norman Walker, and Roy Peratrovich Sr., February 16, 1945. *Alaska State Library. Photo by Amy Lou Blood-Ordway. ASL-P273-1-2.*

14

Carefully Chosen Words

At the end of debate on a bill, it was the custom in the legislature for the Senate president to ask if anyone else wanted to speak. When Senator Edward D. Coffey stood and made that invitation, few in the crowd expected anyone to respond, certainly not the Alaska Native woman with the knitting in her lap. But in the end, Elizabeth was the only one who stepped forward.

Elizabeth took a deep breath. She felt she was ready, but would her words have any effect? She looked at Lori and thought about what kind of life her daughter would have with those ugly signs plastered around town. She thought of the birth mother she never knew, and of her dear adoptive mother, and prickled at the racism they surely must have suffered. She thought of her adoptive father, Andrew, and about how kind he was and how powerful his sermons had been. Words were the tools that had served her all her life, and she and Roy Sr. had spent hours thinking about just the right ones for this occasion. Now was the time.

Elizabeth Peratrovich stood and was acknowledged by the senator. Thirty-three years old and classically styled in white velvet gloves, matching hat, and an olive-green dress, Elizabeth walked slowly down the aisle with her head held high. As she turned to face the assembled legislators, the audience strained forward, pulled by her calm but powerful presence.

If anyone in the room thought the young woman before them would mince her words, they quickly realized their mistake.

"I would not have expected," she began, "that I, who am barely out of savagery, would have to remind gentlemen with five thousand years of recorded civilization behind them of our Bill of Rights." Elizabeth continued in a voice that grew steadier and even more intent. "When my husband and I came to Juneau and sought a home in a nice neighborhood where our children could play happily with our neighbors' children, we found such a house and had arranged to lease it. When the owners learned that we were Indians, they said no. Would we be compelled to live in the slums?"

An often-quoted account of Elizabeth's speech was written by a reporter for the *Daily Alaska Empire* and printed on February 6, 1945. The transcription of Elizabeth's remarks that appears here is similar but is taken from Ernest Gruening's book *Many Battles: The Autobiography of Ernest Gruening.*

Her voice grew louder and clearer. "There are three kinds of persons who practice discrimination against the Indians and other Native people. First, the politician who wants to maintain an inferior minority group so he can always promise them something. Second, the Mr. and Mrs. Jones who aren't quite sure of their social position and who are nice to you on one occasion and can't see you on others, depending on who they are with. Third, the great superman who believes in the superiority of the white race."

Senator Shattuck rose and challenged her, "Will the proposed bill eliminate discrimination?"

Elizabeth answered confidently, "Do your laws against larceny and murder prevent those crimes? No law will eliminate crimes, but at least you as legislators can assert to the world that you recognize the evil of the present situation and speak your intent to help us overcome discrimination."

A long silence seemed to swallow the air in the room. Then a wave of clapping swept through the crowd; even some who had opposed the bill joined in. Cheers rang throughout the gallery and the Senate floor.

Elizabeth made her way back to her seat. She put her arm around her daughter's shoulders as she sat down. She was the last speaker of the day.

When the vote was taken, eleven senators favored the bill, and five voted against it. The legislature of the territory of Alaska passed House Bill 14, Chapter 2, the

Anti-Discrimination Act, providing for "full and equal accommodations, facilities, and privileges to all citizens in places of public accommodations within the jurisdiction of the Territory of Alaska" and specifying penalties for violation.

On February 16, 1945, Governor Ernest Gruening signed the nation's first anti-discrimination bill into law. Not until 1964, nearly twenty years later, did Title VII of the United States Civil Rights Act make it illegal to discriminate on the basis of race or ethnicity throughout the nation.

Elizabeth looked back on that memorable day in her last letter to Roy Jr. when she wrote: "I'll never forget the moment the governor signed the bill, then turned to me, and presented me with the pen with which the bill was signed. The Governor said, 'This is the most important piece of legislation passed in Alaska and will help the most in its development. It never would have passed without your speech.'"

The fighter in velvet gloves had punched more powerfully than any boxer. Yet her only weapon had been her carefully chosen words delivered with elegance and integrity.

The night the bill passed, Elizabeth and Roy Sr. went to the Baranof Hotel, the swankiest establishment in Juneau and one that was previously off-limits to Alaska Native people. Elizabeth wore a stylish taffeta gown, turquoise blue with ruffles at the bodice, and Roy a dashing suit and tie. As the handsome couple approached the dance floor, the others in the room stepped back. But though Elizabeth and Roy were good dancers, that's not why people formed a circle around them. Most everyone, Native and non-Native alike, wanted to celebrate the victory with them.

Roy Jr. was only ten at the time of his mother's famous testimony, and although he doesn't remember the outfit she wore the night his parents celebrated at the Baranof Hotel, he imagines she may have looked as described here.

He later sculpted a bust—now on display at the Smithsonian National Museum of the American Indian and the Alaska State Capitol—depicting his mother in a lovely turquoise gown.

15

What Happened Next

Many things changed after Elizabeth gave her famous testimony. Passage of the anti-discrimination act meant the terrible signs came down, and Alaska Natives gradually moved into neighborhoods where they previously had not been allowed. Schools were integrated and eventually so were clubs like the Rotary and the Elks.

But discrimination did not simply disappear then, nor is it completely gone now. Unfortunately it took years along with well-publicized court cases and fines before some Alaskans realized the law would be enforced. Elizabeth was well aware of these continuing challenges when, in October 1945, she wrote a letter to the National Council of American Indians. She described her fundamental belief that the greatest barrier to equality is ignorance:

We realize its passage will not eliminate Racial Discrimination, but we are satisfied that by the passing of this Bill, our white friends are recognizing that there are discriminations, and they are now interested in correcting this awful injustice. This is a step in the

right direction, and we will continue in our endeavors to
obtain, for our people, rights enjoyed by all.

And so Elizabeth and Roy kept up their work. Elizabeth confronted the local newspaper, the *Daily Alaska Empire*. She asked the editor why he continued to publish the names of young Natives who were suspected of crimes on the front page but buried the names of white suspects in the back of the paper. The editor listened, and soon all juvenile crime reports were handled the same way regardless of race.

Elizabeth went on to help revise the Alaska juvenile code, the laws that apply to children under eighteen. There were many issues that demanded attention. What kind of legal processes are young people entitled to? What kind of punishments are allowed? And what should be done with juvenile criminal records so convicted young people wouldn't be hounded by them for the rest of their lives? Elizabeth was determined to make the Alaska juvenile code non-discriminatory. She tackled it section by section until the inequality was abolished.

Elizabeth also worked with the ANS to promote public-health hospital services for Alaska Native people suffering from tuberculosis. She was elected to the national executive council of the National Congress of American Indians and worked to change its constitution so membership would extend to Alaska Native people who were previously ineligible to join.

Finally, although World War II was over, Elizabeth urged members of the ANB and ANS to contribute to the National War Fund drive in order to "help our boys in the service and for the relief of the starving peoples of the foreign countries of the United Nations."

All the while, Elizabeth somehow managed to care for her own family so well that Roy Jr. later said, "Except for that one instance selling newspapers, I wasn't very aware of the racism Mom and Dad fought so hard against. I was more interested in playing cowboys and Indians, but of course I wanted to be the cowboy."

Still, the thing people remembered most about Elizabeth was her work on the anti-discrimination act. Governor Gruening said of Elizabeth, "her intelligence was obvious, her composure faultless, and her plea could not have been more effective."

Elizabeth Peratrovich,
circa 1950.
*Peratrovich family
photograph collection.*

16

A Quiet Ending

In January of 1957, only a dozen years after Elizabeth's famous testimony, Roy Jr., by then a student at the University of Washington majoring in engineering, received his mother's final letter. Written in her clear, graceful style, the letter explained how she felt about her long struggle for equality:

> *Rich and poor, strong and weak gave their help in this difficult fight. All this without hate, notoriety, or malice. Finally, Alaska pulled herself out of her deep unnecessary sleep and the laws began to change. Why? Because people were awakened to their obligation to their fellow men.*

She talked about what it means to know you are on the side of justice.

> *A few times some people tried to discriminate against us but that is almost impossible to do when the object of such action feels no inferiority.*

She ended with something Roy Jr. did not fully understand until later.

My own selfishness, and I must call it that, is due to the fact that I do live on borrowed time. Please forgive me for this my dears. I must have more faith.

Love, Mother

P.S. Daddy adds his love and blessing. Write us as often as you can.

A year after the letter to Roy Jr., Elizabeth was admitted to the Christian Science Care Facility in Seattle with breast cancer. Just as she had prepared herself to fight for equality for Alaska Natives, Elizabeth steeled herself for a different battle, but one she would not win.

Roy Jr., who had recently married and graduated from the University of Washington with a degree in civil engineering, was working in Seattle. He visited his mother every day and witnessed her increasing frailty. Though she grew terribly thin and suffered greatly, Elizabeth asked Roy Jr. not to tell his father how sick she was. Roy Sr. was in Juneau working and watching over Lori, who was about to graduate from high school. Elizabeth didn't want her husband to worry, and she wanted him to remember her not as a patient, but as the strong partner she had always been.

In June of 1958, Elizabeth held Roy Jr.'s first child–her first grandchild–in her arms. She died six months later on December 1, at the age of forty-seven. Roy Sr. outlived her by thirty-one years and died in 1989. Their spirits, however, live on, inhabiting the most important individual right in Alaska or anywhere: the right to equal treatment under the law, no more, no less.

Epilogue

In 1988 Alaska governor Steve Cowper proclaimed February 16 as Elizabeth Peratrovich Day for all of Alaska. It was not because Elizabeth was the only one who worked for Native rights; many others worked, and many are still working, to battle the evils of racism and discrimination. Rather, the day is an annual reminder of what Elizabeth called our "obligation to our fellow men." Over the years it has become, to some, a celebration of what it means to be Alaska Native.

Gallery B of the Alaska State Capitol, where Elizabeth gave her stirring testimony, was named in her honor on May 1, 1992. Fran Ulmer, then a member of the Alaska House of Representatives and later lieutenant governor of Alaska, said at the dedication, "In naming Gallery B for Elizabeth, we honor her today for her vision, her wisdom, and her courage in speaking out for what she believed to be right. She symbolizes the role the gallery plays in the legislature and the importance of public opinion in the legislative process. She reminds us that a single person, speaking from the heart, can affect the future of all Alaskans."

Governor Steve Cowper first proclaimed Elizabeth Peratrovich Day
in 1988. The date of the celebration was later changed from April 21
to February 16.
Alaska State Library Historical Collection.

Elizabeth Peratrovich sculpted in bronze, by Roy Peratrovich Jr. On display at the Alaska State Capital and Smithsonian National Museum of the American Indian. *Peratrovich family photograph collection.*

Elizabeth's daughter Lori had this to say about the designation of Elizabeth Peratrovich Day:

> My mom would probably say Roy should be here with me [being honored]. And you know what my dad would say? It was all your mother. They were strictly a team. Dad was right alongside her; it was never just mother. They complemented each other. What one thought, the other usually just felt the same way. They backed each other up and said, "Let's do it."

Roy Jr. sculpted a bust of Elizabeth based on his vision of what his mother might have worn when she and Roy Sr. celebrated at the Baranof Hotel. He made a bust of his father as well. The sculpture of his mother is on display at the Alaska State Capitol Building and both sculptures are on display at the Smithsonian National Museum in Washington DC.

In 2001 Alaskan Tlingit actress and writer Diane Benson, Lxeis', wrote, produced, and performed in a one-act play entitled, *When My Spirit Raised Its Hands: The Story of Elizabeth Peratrovich and Alaska Civil Rights*. The play toured throughout Alaska's schools. In 2009 Benson again played the role of Elizabeth Peratrovich in a feature-length docudrama, *For the Rights of All: Ending Jim Crow in Alaska*, that aired on PBS stations nationwide. The film was produced by Alaska filmmaker Jeffry Silverman of Blueberry Productions.

In February 2003, the Roy and Elizabeth Peratrovich Park on Fourth and E Streets in Anchorage was dedicated to honor the couple's efforts and accomplishments.

On June 30, 2008, *The Flight of the Raven*, a bronze sculpture created by Roy Peratrovich Jr. to honor his parents and others for their work in support of equal rights legislation, was unveiled at the Roy and Elizabeth Peratrovich Park. Roy Jr. explained that his sculpture was a futuristic totem pole, a reminder of how his parents helped Alaska soar to new heights.

On February 16, 2017, the U.S. Forest Service and the Alaska Native Brotherhood and Sisterhood named the theater in the Southeast Alaska Discovery Center in Ketchikan, Alaska, in honor of Elizabeth Peratrovich. The event coincided with the annual Elizabeth Peratrovich Day celebration organized by the ANB/ANS Camps 14 (Ketchikan) and 15 (Saxman).

Roy Peratrovich Jr. and *The Flight of the Raven*, Roy and Elizabeth Peratrovich Park, Anchorage Municipality, 2008. *Peratrovich family photograph collection.*

Finally, in 2017, the U.S. Mint announced that Elizabeth Peratrovich, the fighter in velvet gloves, would make one more public appearance, this time gracing a commemorative one-dollar coin. Just like Elizabeth Peratrovich Day, the coin (minted in 2020) will honor not only the Peratrovich name but the Tlingit nation, Alaska Native people, and indeed all Native Americans.

TOP AND MIDDLE
The Peratrovich
gravesites, Evergreen
Cemetery, Juneau.
Photos by the author.

BOTTOM
12th Street Peratrovich
Family Home, Juneau.
Photo by the author.

Afterword

On a beautiful spring day in Juneau, I went on a treasure hunt with my dog, ZZ. I had two stars on my map: The gravesite of Elizabeth and Roy Peratrovich Sr. and the house on 12th Street, where the Peratrovich family lived in later years.

In the Evergreen Cemetery I trudged back and forth near where I thought the gravesite might be. I was about to give up when ZZ led me to the headstones, side by side, as the couple was in life. Roy Peratrovich Sr., May 1, 1908–February 7, 1989 (two days past the forty-fourth anniversary of his wife's famous testimony in the Territorial Alaska Legislature) and Elizabeth Jean Peratrovich, July 4, 1911–December 1, 1958 (just thirteen years after her testimony).

The house at 644 West 12th Street, built long ago by a Norwegian fisherman, was an easy find. It is an unassuming two-story home sandwiched between others with yards not much wider than the sidewalk and on a street that has seen countless lives come and go since Juneau's first mines were dug in the late 1800s.

I paused and gazed at the little blue house, wondering if the people who live there today realize they are on hallowed ground. Do they know of the work that went on inside those walls? Do they know that an ordinary family with extraordinary ideas and determination lived there while they helped change the lives of every Alaskan for the better?

The story of Elizabeth Peratrovich is a personal one for me. Juneau was a small town of about ten thousand people in the 1950s, when I was growing up there. As I researched this book, I was surprised to discover how many of the individuals in Elizabeth's story intersected my life. Many were family friends or neighbors. In fact, it was my niece, Hilary Lindh, who introduced me to Roy Peratrovich Jr., and that was the start of this book because I never would have attempted it without Roy!

Hilary was working for the Alaska State Department of Transportation in 2014 when the old Brotherhood Bridge in Juneau was being replaced by a new one. Roy Jr., the first Alaska Native certified as a civil engineer in Alaska, worked on the design of the original bridge, which was named after the Alaska Native Brotherhood in honor of the organization's fiftieth anniversary. Hilary had contacted him for help in moving a series of decorative bronze medallions he had also designed from the railing of the old bridge to the new one.

As a former librarian and teacher in Juneau, I had long wished for a book about Elizabeth Peratrovich that

Author Annie
Boochever and Roy
Peratrovich Jr., 2015.
*Photograph by Roy's wife,
Toby Peratrovich,
in their back yard.*

was accessible to younger readers. When Roy said he would help me document his mother's legacy, I was thrilled. Roy provided a wealth of resources and personal stories. He even remembers delivering newspapers to my own family's house. And he recalls seeing my dad, an attorney and later a judge, but more importantly a basketball enthusiast, like nearly everyone in Alaska, at the Gold Medal Basketball Tournaments in Juneau.

One of the heroes in this story is territorial governor Ernest Gruening. My father was a great admirer of Governor Gruening, and I have vivid memories of family dinners that included the governor and his wife, Dorothy. The Gruening's son, Hunt, and his children—Bradford, Winford, and Clark—grew up in the house right behind us and often played with my sisters and me. We called them "those Gruening boys."

My parents moved to Juneau in 1946, so they narrowly missed the anti-discrimination bill hearing. Had they been there, they would have been fervent supporters. My dad practiced law in Juneau for many years before becoming an Alaska Supreme Court justice. In 1980 he was appointed by President Jimmy Carter to the Ninth Circuit Court of Appeals. He became well-known for opinions that valued equal rights, especially for the underserved. He was particularly concerned about the racism he witnessed in Juneau.

One of my childhood friends was Anna "Sugie" Paddock, who lived just down the street. Neither she nor I knew at the time that Elizabeth Peratrovich was her aunt.

Finally, Shell Simmons and his wife, Marge, lived right across the street from my family. We often visited them, but I never got to ride in the Grumman Goose.

Timeline

1864   William H. Paddock, Elizabeth's birth father, is born July 15 in Union, Indiana. He died March 14, 1927, in Tennakee, Alaska.

1867   United States purchased Alaska from Russia.

1876   Anna Tagcook Paddock, William H. Paddock's wife, is born in Haines. She died February 1, 1952, in Juneau.

1884   Edith Tagcook Paul, Elizabeth's birth mother, is born in Haines. She died April 1943 in Juneau.

1884   Organic Act is passed by the United States Congress.

1884   Jean Williams Wanamaker, Elizabeth's adoptive mother, is born August 8, in Sitka. She died November 28, 1941, in Juneau.

1886   Andrew Jack Wanamaker, Elizabeth's adoptive father, is born January 11, in Sitka. He died May 13, 1969, in Sitka.

1908   Roy Peratrovich, Elizabeth's husband, is born May 1, in Klawock. He died February 7, 1989, in Juneau.

1910   Edith Tagcook Paul takes care of her sister Anna's children while their mother is convalescing from tuberculosis at a Juneau sanatorium.

1911   Elizabeth Jean Wanamaker is born to Edith Tagcook Paul on July 4, in Petersburg.

1911–   Elizabeth, Andrew, and Jean Wanamaker live in
1931   Sitka, Ketchikan, and Klawock.

1912   Second Organic Act is passed by Congress.

1912   Alaska Native Brotherhood is formed.

1915   Alaska Native Sisterhood is founded by a group of women in Wrangell.

1924   U.S. Congress passes the Indian Citizenship Act that grants citizenship to all Native Americans and Alaska Natives.

1928–   Roy attends the Chemawa Indian School in
1930   Salem, Oregon.

1930   Elizabeth briefly attends Sheldon Jackson Boarding High School in Sitka.

1931   Roy and Elizabeth graduate from Ketchikan High School.

1931   Roy and Elizabeth attend Bellingham Normal School (Western Washington University) for one quarter.

1931   Roy and Elizabeth are married on December 15 in Bellingham.

1931– Roy and Elizabeth live in Klawock and start a
1941 family. Roy joins the Alaska Native Brotherhood and Elizabeth joins the Alaska Native Sisterhood.

1939 Ernest Gruening appointed governor of the Territory of Alaska.

1940 Roy is elected grand president of the ANB and Elizabeth is elected grand vice president of the ANS.

1941 Roy, Elizabeth, and their children–Roy Jr., Frank, and Loretta–move to Juneau.

1943 The territorial legislature considers the state anti-discrimination bill for the first time, and it is defeated.

1944 Alberta Schenck, an Alaska Native, is jailed in Nome for sitting with her white date, a U.S. Army sergeant, in the Nome Dream Theater's whites-only section.

1945 On February 5, Elizabeth–now grand president of the ANS–addresses the Territorial Senate during its debate on the anti-discrimination bill.

1945 On February 16, territorial governor Ernest Gruening signs the Alaska Anti-Discrimination Act of 1945 into law.

1952 Roy Sr. moves to Nova Scotia, Canada to pursue a degree in economics at St. Francis Xavier University.

1955   Elizabeth becomes a member of the executive
        committee of the National Congress of American
        Indians.

1956   While in Tenessee attending a conference
        on adult education, Elizabeth hears Martin
        Luther King Jr. speak about the desegregation
        of churches. According to her family, he made
        quite an impression on her.

1958   Elizabeth dies in Seattle on December 1.

1959   January 3, President Eishenhour signs the official
        declaration making Alaska the 49th state of the
        United States of America.

1982   The ANB designates Roy Sr. Grand President
        Emeritus.

1988   On April 21, SB499 was passed, designating
        February 16 as Elizabeth Peratrovich Day
        beginning in 1989.

1992   On May 1, Gallery B in the Alaska State Capitol
        is renamed the "Elizabeth Peratrovich Gallery"
        in Elizabeth's honor.

2003   In February, a park in downtown Anchorage
        is named for Roy and Elizabeth Peratrovich.
        It encompasses the lawn surrounding
        Anchorage's former city hall and includes a
        small amphitheater where concerts and other
        performances are held.

2008   On June 30, *The Flight of the Raven*, a bronze, stainless steel, and quartz sculpture by Roy Peratrovich Jr., is unveiled at the park in Anchorage to honor his parents and others for their work in support of equal rights legislation.

2009   On October 22, *For the Rights of All: Ending Jim Crow in Alaska*, a documentary about Elizabeth Peratrovich's groundbreaking civil rights journey, premiers at the Alaska Federation of Natives convention in Anchorage. It airs on PBS stations in November 2009.

2017   On February 16, the theater in Ketchikan's Southeast Alaska Discovery Center is named in honor of Elizabeth Peratrovich, and a companion exhibit exploring her role in the struggle for Alaska Native civil rights is unveiled.

2017   On June 30, the U.S. Mint announces a new one-dollar coin with designs honoring Elizabeth Peratrovich and the landmark anti-discrimination law. The coin is scheduled for release in 2020.

2018   Elizabeth Peratrovich is chosen by the National Women's History Project as an honoree for Women's History Month in the United States.

Glossary

assimilate To absorb and integrate people, ideas, or culture into a wider society or another culture. Assimilation of Alaska Native culture into Western culture was U.S. policy from the late 1800s into the 1940s. That meant obliterating traditional languages, cultural knowledge, and practices and replacing them with those derived from western Europe. Reverend Sheldon Jackson was perhaps the best-known proponent of assimilation during Alaska's territorial days.

clan A division or smaller group of a moiety. Each clan has its own stories, songs, and totems; and each forms a social network of extended families that functions as a political unit in Tlingit society.

discrimination The unjust or prejudicial treatment of groups of people or things. Current federal law prohibits discriminating against individuals on the basis of race, color, religion, sex, or national origin. A few states have moved to include sexual orientation as well.

1884 Alaska Organic Act When the United States purchased the land that would become Alaska from Russia in 1867, the population of the entire area was about thirty-one thousand Alaska Native people and about nine hundred whites (the latter of which mainly lived in Sitka). Because of the small population, the U.S. government didn't feel a need to establish a local system of government. It wasn't until 1884 that residents of Alaska convinced Washington, DC, that some form of local government was necessary to develop the state's extensive resources. The 1884 Organic Act allowed Alaska to become a judicial district as well as a civil one, with an appointed governor, judges, clerks, marshals, and other federal officials. However, the act did not go so far as to designate Alaska an official territory of the United States.

gumboots A type of marine mollusk found in tidal and subtidal zones. Shaaw (its Tlingit name) provides essential vitamins and minerals especially important for a subsistence lifestyle. They are eaten raw, boiled, steamed, pickled, or roasted. Also called black leather chiton.

Indian boarding schools Developed to direct and accelerate the assimilation of American Indian and Alaska Native children. Conditions at the boarding schools were often substandard, and many children were malnourished, which left them vulnerable to a host of diseases. When students became extremely sick, the schools tried to send them home, but children who died were often buried in the schools' own cemeteries—sometimes in unmarked graves. Sadly, families were not always informed of these deaths. By 1900 thousands of Native Americans were studying at nearly 150 boarding schools around the United States. The schools insisted that students stop using their Indian names and cut their long hair. Speaking Native languages was forbidden.

Indian Citizenship Act of 1924 Prior to this act, some Native Americans were citizens by virtue of a particular treaty or because they had served in the armed forces, but there was no path to citizenship that applied to all Native Americans. The act granted citizenship to all Native Americans born in the United States or in a U.S. territory (such as Alaska). It did not require people to apply or give up their tribal membership to become U.S. citizens.

Ḵu.éex' An important event honoring a deceased loved one, the raising of a totem pole, or the dedication of a house. The celebration features speeches, dancing, singing, feasting, and the generous distribution of gifts and property. The English word for *Ḵu.éex'* is *potlatch,* which means "to give."

lay minister A term for members of faiths (typically Christian denominations) who are not full-time or ordained clergy but who perform similar functions.

Stella Martin Martin, whose Tlingit name is Yaan da yein, was born on November 28, 1922, in Kake to Charles and Annie Johnson. She was of the Tsaagweidei, Killer Whale Clan, of the Yellow Cedar House (Xaai Hit') and the Eagle moiety. She served two terms as grand president of the ANS Grand Camp, and at the time of her death in September 2002, she held the honored title of grand president emeritus. Martin was active in the Salvation Army, Central Council Tlingit and Haida Indian Tribes of Alaska (CCTHITA), the St. Ann's Hospital board, Sealaska Heritage Institute, and the Alaska Legal Services board, among other civic organizations.

She was also one of the first tribal judges, an AWARE (Aiding Women in Abuse and Rape Emergencies) Woman of Distinction, a Sealaska Woman of the Year, winner of the Elizabeth Peratrovich ANS Citizenship Award, and a Delegate of the Year for CCTHITA.

moeity Social or ritual groups into which a people are divided. The two moieties in Tlingit society are Raven (Yéil) and Eagle (Ch'áak'). All Tlingit people are members of one or the other.

William Lewis Paul Sr. Paul's Tlingit name was Shgúndi. He was born May 7, 1885, in Tongass Village, Alaska, and died March 4, 1977, in Seattle. He and his brother, Louis Paul (1887–1956), are considered foundational members of the Alaska Native Brotherhood. William Paul Sr. was the first Alaska Native to become an attorney, the first to be elected to the Alaska Territorial House of Representatives, and the first to serve as an officer in the federal Bureau of Indian Affairs. He played a major role in the Alaska Native Claims Settlement Act of 1971.

Roy Peratrovich Jr. The eldest son of Elizabeth Peratrovich and Roy Peratrovich Sr., Roy Jr. was born in Klawock, Alaska, in 1934 and given the Tlingit name Yéil Nah Hoo (meaning a Raven Chief). He was the first Alaska Native to be registered as a professional civil engineer in Alaska and co-founded the engineering firm Peratrovich, Nottingham, and Drage in 1979. Prior to that, he worked for the Alaska State Department of Transportation and helped design the 1965 Brotherhood Bridge in Juneau. The bridge honored the Alaska Native Brotherhood and symbolized the bridging of the gap between Native and non-Native Alaskans. Roy Jr. also designed ten large bronze medallions representing the Raven and Eagle moieties for the bridge. The medallions were reinstalled in the pedestrian railing of the new Brotherhood Bridge dedicated in October 2015. After his retirement, Roy Jr. worked as a full-time artist. At the age of eighty-one, Roy wrote *Little Whale: A Story of the Last Tlingit War Canoe*, published by University of Alaska Press in 2016.

regalia Special clothes and decorations, especially those used at official ceremonies. Regalia used by Southeast Alaska Native people typically displays power, wealth, and lineage. It is an acknowledgment of the ancestors who came before. The maker is important and is typically a member of a different clan. Some examples of traditional Tlingit regalia are button blankets, ceremonial hats, Chilkat robes, and Raven's Tail robes.

Second Organic Act (1912) Almost thirty years after the 1884 Organic Act, Congress passed the second Organic Act, which created the U.S. territory of Alaska and the territorial legislature. The territory included four judicial districts, each with twenty-four elected representatives and two senators. The first twenty-four territorial legislators hailed from Candle, Douglas, Fairbanks, Fox, Iditarod, Juneau, Katalla, Ketchikan, Knik, Nome, Ruby, Seward, Sitka, Skagway, Valdez, and Wrangell. All were men, and none were Alaska Native.

Sheldon "Shell" Simmons A legendary bush pilot and airline pioneer. Born in Idaho in 1908, he moved to Alaska and bought a damaged airplane for one dollar to start his first flying business, Alaska Air Transport. Years later, after a storied history filled with often heroic adventures, his company, Alaska Coastal Airlines, became part of the Alaska Airlines we know today. He served on the Alaska Airlines Board of Directors for many years and died in 1994 at age eighty-six.

segregation The enforced separation or isolation of different racial, religious, or cultural groups in a country, community, or establishment.

statehood Alaska became the forty-ninth state in 1959 after an arduous battle led by territorial governor Ernest Gruening. Much of this story is chronicled in Gruening's autobiography, *Many Battles: The Autobiography of Ernest Gruening.*

subsistence In Alaska, a subsistence lifestyle relies on hunting, fishing, and gathering to provide for basic needs. (In other areas, farming may also be considered a subsistence activity, but that is not typically the way the word is used in Alaska.) For thousands of years, Alaska Natives obtained everything they needed to survive through subsistence activities. Even today, residents of many rural villages have limited access to grocery stores and get most of their food this way. In larger cities, many Alaskans organize their annual schedules around hunting, fishing, and berry-picking seasons, and many consider this to be "subsistence." In this book, subsistence refers to the hunting, fishing, and gathering as the primary source of food.

territorial government Alaska was a U.S. territory from 1912 until 1959, when it became a state. In a territory, the governor is appointed, rather than elected, by the president of the United States. Territories have no representatives in the U.S. Congress. For more information, see "How a Territory Differs from a State" from *Statehood for Alaska: The Issues Involved and the Facts about the Issues* by George Sundborg Sr.

Tlingit language According to the University of Alaska Fairbank's Alaska Native Language Center, Tlingit is the language of coastal Southeast Alaska Natives from Yakutat south to Ketchikan. Out of a population of approximately ten thousand Tlingits in sixteen communities, there are about five hundred Tlingit language speakers. Thanks to the documentation, preservation, and cultural education programs throughout Southeast Alaska, the language is experiencing a revitalization.

Tlingit is a complicated language with many sounds that English doesn't have, for example, the voiceless *L*. Try this: Say *LLL*. Keep your tongue in the same place and breathe in. Feel the cold air at the sides of your tongue? Now, still keeping your tongue in the same place, blow out and in. When you blow out, that's the voiceless *L*. You're pronouncing an *L* without your voice, just with your breath! Now try to use the voiceless *L* to say *Gunalchéesh*, pronounced *Goon a(l) cheesh* or "thank you" in Tlingit. (Courtesy of Alice Taff, PhD, affiliate assistant professor of Alaska Native languages, University of Alaska Southeast).

Bibliography

Alaska Legislative Centennial Commission. *Alaska State Legislature Roster of Members: Centennial Edition, 1913–2013.* Juneau: Legislative Affairs Agency, 2013. http://w3.legis.state.ak.us/docs/pdf/ROM-centennial.pdf.

Alaska Native Brotherhood Alaska Native Sisterhood Grand Camp. https://www.anbansgc.org/about-us/.

Alaska Women's Hall of Fame. "Alberta Schenck Daisy Adams" http://alaskawomenshalloffame.org/alumnae/class-of-2010.

Bowman, Nick. "Ketchikan Theater Named for Elizabeth Peratrovich," *Ketchikan Daily News.* February 17, 2017, http://juneauempire.com/state/2017-02-17/ketchikan-theater-named-elizabeth-peratrovich.

Central Council. *A Recollection of Civil Rights Leader Elizabeth Peratrovich, 1911–1958.* Juneau: Central Council of Tlingit and Haida Indian Tribes of Alaska, 1991.

"Citizenship: United States, State of Alaska, Tribal."
In *Federal Indian Law for Alaska Tribes*, Unit 2.
Tribal Management 112. University of Alaska
Fairbanks. http://tribalmgmt.uaf.edu/tm112/Unit-2/
Citizenship-United-States-State-of-Alaska-Tribal.

"Clans and Moieties." Social Studies, grade 6, unit 7,
Juneau: Sealaska Heritage Institute. sealaskaheritage.
org/sites/default/files/Unit%207_2.pdf.

Cochrane, Marjorie. "Elizabeth Peratrovich: 'The
Martin Luther King of Alaska.'" In *Bold Women in
Alaska History*, 73–87. Missoula, MT: Mountain Press
Publishing Company, 2014.

Dadigan, Marc. "Unmarked Graves Discovered at
Chemawa Indian School." Aljazeera, January 3,
2016. https://www.aljazeera.com/indepth/
features/2016/01/unearthing-dark-native-boarding-
school-160103072842972.html.

Dauenhauer, Nora Marks, and Richard Dauenhauer.
Haa Kusteeyí, Our Culture: Tlingit Life Stories. Seattle:
University of Washington Press, 1994.

Fletcher, Amy. "Tlingit Civil Rights Hero William Paul
Sr. Remembered," *Juneau Empire*, May 13, 2015.
http://juneauempire.com/art/2015-05-13/tlingit-
civil-rights-hero-william-paul-sr-remembered.

Gruening, Ernest. *Many Battles: The Autobiography of
Ernest Gruening*. New York: Liveright, 1973.

Juneau Retired Teachers Association. *Juneau Teacher Tales, 1930s–1950s.* 2nd ed. Juneau: Juneau Retired Educators Association, 2014.

History Matters: The U.S. Survey Course on the Web. "Kill the Indian, and Save the Man": Capt. Richard H. Pratt on the Education of Native Americans. http://historymatters.gmu.edu/d/4929/.

"Interview with Roy Peratrovich, 1988. Parts I, II, III and IV," in Alaska Native Storyteller, a blog by Ishmael Hope. February 26, 2011. Interview by Sealaska Heritage Institute and the University of Alaska Fairbanks, Project Jukebox series. Zachary Jones, archivist/historian. http://alaskanativestoryteller.com/blog/page/16/.

Kiffer, Dave. "For 30 Years, Ellis and Alaska Coastal Were the Only Way to Fly in Southeast," *SitNews Stories in the News*, Ketchikan, Alaska, June 20, 2018. http://www.sitnews.us/Kiffer/AlaskaCoastal/062018_alaska_coastal.html.

La Belle, Jim, Stacy L. Smith, Cheryl Easley, and Kanaqlak (George P. Charles), eds. "Boarding School: Historical Trauma among Alaska's Native People." National Resource Center for American Indian, Alaska Native, and Native Hawaiian Elders. University of Alaska Anchorage, January 2006. http://docplayer.net/14331501-National-resource-center-for-american-indian-alaska-native-and-native-hawaiian-elders.html.

Lundborg, Murray. Introduction to "The 1884 Alaska Organic Act." *Explore North: An Explorer's Guide to the North.* http://www.explorenorth.com/library/yafeatures/bl-Alaska1884.htm.

Metcalfe, Kimberly L., ed. *In Sisterhood: The History of Camp 2 of the Alaska Native Sisterhood.* Juneau, AK: Hazy Island Books, 2008.

"Native Arts." Social studies, grade 6, unit 9. Juneau: Sealaska Heritage Institute. sealaskaheritage.org/sites/default/file/Unit%209_3.pdf.

Oleksa, Michael J. "Elizabeth W. Peratrovich, Tlingit Indian Civil Rights Activist (1911–1958)." In *Six Alaskan Native Women Leaders: Pre-Statehood*, edited by Connie Munro and Anne Kessler. Juneau: Alaska State Department of Education, 1991. https://files.eric.ed.gov/fulltext/ED377992.pdf.

"100 Years of Alaska's Legislature: 'From Territorial Days to Today, 1913–2013: Percy Ipalook.'" http://w3.legis.state.ak.us/100years/bio.php?id=1192.

Silverman, Jeffry Lloyd, producer. *For the Rights of All: Ending Jim Crow in Alaska.* Anchorage: Blueberry Productions, 2008.

Sitka Art blog (Sitkabecca). "The Oral History of Sheldon Jackson School and College." April 8, 2014. https://sitkaartblog.wordpress.com/2014/04/08/a-brief-chronology-of-sheldon-jackson-school-and-college/.

"Stella Martin," Obituary. *Juneau Empire.* August 30, 2002. juneauempire.com/stories/083002/loc_martin.shtml.

Sundborg, George, Sr. "How a Territory Differs from a State." In *Statehood for Alaska: The Issues Involved and the Facts about the Issues.* Anchorage: Alaska Statehood Association, 1946. https://www.alaska.edu/creatingalaska/statehood-files/territory-differs-from-st/.

"Super Race Theory Hit in Hearing," *Daily Alaska Empire.* February 6, 1945. http://vilda.alaska.edu/cdm/ref/collection/cdmg21/id/2058.

"Tlingit." Alaska Native Language Center, University of Alaska Fairbanks. https://www.uaf.edu/anlc/languages/tl/.

Tlingit, Haida, and Tsimshian Genealogy of Canada and Alaska. Updated December 20, 2017. Entry 63290. https://wc.rootsweb.ancestry.com/cgibin/igm.cgi?op=GET&db=klea&id=I5759.

Waterbury, Barbara. "Tlingit Potlaches." Sheldon Museum and Cultural Center, Haines, Alaska. 1987. Updated and revised by Blythe Carter, 2013. http://www.sheldonmuseum.org/vignettes/tlingit-potlatches.

Acknowledgments

This story could not have been told without the support and assistance of Elizabeth's son, Roy Jr., Yéil Nah Hoo. Roy provided family information and documents that would not otherwise have been available. More than that, his personal remembrances of his mother and his experiences growing up are the basis for much of the book. I am grateful to him for allowing me to use parts of the 1957 letter he received from his mother as well as the poem she wrote to her friend in 1931.

I feel particularly indebted to the Central Council of Tlingit and Haida Indian Tribes of Alaska (CCTHITA) and staff members Wanda Culp and Sharon Olsen. In 1991 they had the foresight to produce *A Recollection of Civil Rights Leader Elizabeth Peratrovich, 1911–1958* when many of those involved in the passage of the anti-discrimination bill were still available to interview and question.

betsy Peratrovich (who lowercases her first name), Shaaxaatk'í, a granddaughter of Elizabeth Peratrovich and herself an activist for equal rights, reviewed multiple drafts of the book and made invaluable suggestions.

Many others provided guidance, particularly with respect to Tlingit language and customs and other Alaska historical information. They include Lance Twitchell, Xh'unei, assistant professor of Alaska Native languages, University of Alaska Southeast; Alice Taff, PhD, affiliate assistant professor of Alaska Native languages, University of Alaska Southeast; Hans Chester, Naakil.-aan, Tlingit language and culture teacher; Rosita Worl, PhD, Tlingit names Yeidiklasókw and Kaaháni, president of the Sealaska Heritage Institute and assistant professor of anthropology at the University of Alaska Southeast; Pamela Cravez, JD, editor of the *Alaska Justice Forum* and research associate at the University of Alaska Anchorage Justice Center; Averil Lerman, JD, legal historian; and Marie Williams Olson, Kaajeexán, Tlingit Elder, cultural advocate, educator, and three-term ANS Camp 2 president, who graciously sat with me and answered many questions about her life growing up in Juneau.

Throughout this book, historical photographs have been used to help document the story. Roy Jr. generously provided portions of his private family collection as well as a rare photo of Elizabeth's birth family given to him by Maxine Richert, with permission for use in this book by Tom and Sarah Paddock. Also, I am grateful for Elizabeth's birth mother's story given to me by Maxine Richert.

Other photographs were obtained with the support and assistance of the staff at the Alaska State Library Historical Collections, especially Anastasia Tarmann, librarian and project director, and Tanya Stepanova, former state archivist.

Much appreciation to the University of Alaska Press, including the acquisition committee, for believing in the project and to Elizabeth Laska, assistant editor, and Krista West, production editor, for their technical help and patient support.

Finally, thank you to my family for their encouragement and advice (lots of advice).

About the Author

Annie Boochever grew up in Juneau in the days when Alaska was still a territory. Racism, although subtler than before passage of the anti-discrimination bill, was still pervasive. Even as a child, she was painfully aware of it.

Annie worked as an educator in Alaska and in Newtown, Connecticut, where she was named Weller Foundation Teacher of the Year. To promote understanding between cultures, she wrote and produced more than a dozen multicultural musical plays for elementary students to perform for their communities. Annie also co-founded the Alaska Children's Theater and taught high school English and graduate-level teaching courses as well as classroom music and library.

Annie earned an MFA in Creative Writing for Children and Young Adults from the Northwest Institute of Literary Arts. Her first book, *Bristol Bay Summer* (Alaska Northwest Books, 2014), was an Alaska State Battle of the Books selection for middle-grades and won an International Literary Classic's award for best first novel.

Now retired from teaching, Annie writes and loves to swim, ski, play piano, and garden. She recently moved to Bellingham, Washington, where she lives with her husband and a Dutch dog of dazzling emotional intelligence named ZZ.